Strawb

M000043233

by Taneesha Campbell
illustrated by John Kurtz

HOUGHTON MIFFLIN   BOSTON

Printed in China

ISBN 10: 0-618-88662-1
ISBN 13: 978-0-618-88662-3

23456789 SDP 16 15 14 13 12 11 10 09 08

Grandpa wanted strawberries.
He wanted lots of berries.
He asked Tina and Theo to
get some.

Tina had I bucket full.

So did Theo.

Each bucket had 10 berries.

How many berries did they pick?

Tina kept on picking.
Theo kept on picking.
They filled 4 buckets.

Now how many berries did they pick?

Tina filled 2 more buckets.
Theo filled 2 more buckets.
They now had 4 buckets each.

How many berries did they pick?

They picked 2 more buckets.
Then they were done.
Tina and Theo started home.

How many berries are in the wagon?

They gave Grandpa the berries.
Tina and Theo gave him 5 buckets.
Grandpa ate one berry.
"Mmm. These will make a
good pie."

How many berries did each fox give him?

Buckets of Berries

Draw
Look at page 5. Draw the buckets you see in the wagon.

Tell About
Look at page 5. Tell how many buckets of strawberries the foxes picked. Tell how many berries they have in all.

Write
Draw Conclusions Look at page 5. Write how many strawberries the foxes picked in all.